Terrific Teddy's Excessive Energy

By Jim Forgan, Ph.D.
Illustrated by Rob Barge

Copyright © 2015 by Jim Forgan, Ph.D.

All rights reserved. No portion of this book may be reproduced, stored in a retrieval system, or transmitted in any form or by any means – electronic, mechanical, photocopy, recording, scanning, or other – except for brief quotations in critical reviews or articles, without the prior written permission of the publisher. For permission requests, write to Advocacy Consultants Press, 641 University Boulevard, Suite 114, Jupiter FL 33458.

Terrific Teddy™ is a trademark of Jim Forgan, Ph.D.; Advocacy Consultants Press; and/or its subsidiaries in the United States and/or other countries.

Published by Advocacy Consultants Press
Printed in the United States of America

Edited, art-directed and designed by Jodi MacNeal (www.jodimacneal.com)

Publisher's Cataloging-in-Publication data

Forgan, Jim, Ph.D.
Terrific teddy's excessive energy / written by Jim Forgan, Ph.D. / illustrated by Rob Barge
p. cm.

ISBN: 978-0-9862796-5-2
1. Attention - deficit hyperactivity disorder – Juvenile literature. 2. Learning differences – Juvenile literature.

Hello.

I am a school psychologist and I specialize in assessing children for ADHD/ADD, dyslexia, dysgraphia, and other learning differences. When I sit down with parents to review their child's testing results, I make sure to ask, "What will you tell your child about the results?" I do this because I want parents to be prepared to have a conversation that won't frighten, confuse or discourage their child. I wrote this book based not only on the discussions I've had with clients, but also on personal experience as a parent explaining learning differences to my own child.

This book helps you explain learning differences so children can grasp why self-control, focus, and remembering can be so hard. Children benefit from books like this for several reasons. First, children need to know they're not alone. Second, it places boundaries around a child's weaker areas. It's a reminder that it's only his or her *behavior* that needs work – not their entire being. Third, your child understands why you will be providing extra support.

As you read to your child, here are some tips to enhance your time together:
(a) Allow your child to sit on your lap or next to you as you read the book together.
(b) Read the entire book to your child; don't require the child to read at all. We want the child to absorb the ideas, not fret about figuring out the words.
(c) Periodically pause to discuss the book's ideas.
(d) Discuss what you like about the book's character.
(e) Discuss how the book's concepts relate to your child and family.

The last page of the story contains two optional endings. Some parents don't want to use the term ADHD with their child and may choose the first option. Other parents are more straightforward, and I've written the second ending for those who want their children to understand the term ADHD. This is a matter of personal preference, but my recommendation is to discuss ADHD by name by the time your child completes third grade.

Your child is fortunate to have you. Keep the faith.
Jim Forgan, Ph.D.

I'm Teddy.

I move around a lot.

My head tells me to sit still. But my body doesn't always listen.

"Teddy, I want you to sit on your bottom, in your chair, with all four legs and both of your feet flat on the floor," my teacher said.

I really tried.

My head tells me to keep quiet. But my mouth doesn't always listen.

"Teddy, stop that singing," said Sara. "Yeah," said Jack. "You make too many noises. I can't think when you do that."

I really tried.

My head tells me to pay attention to my teacher. But my ears don't always listen.

When it's time to line up for lunch, I'm not always ready. "It's too bad Teddy's making poor choices," my teacher said, "because now his group will line up last."

"Not again!" my classmates cried. "Now we're last for the third day in a row."

I was really sorry.

On the way to the cafeteria to eat lunch, I suddenly felt like Superman and started to fly through the hallway with my cape fluttering behind me.

"Teddy!" My teacher was using her serious voice. "Walk quietly with your hands by your side. I've about had it with your behavior and I am going to call your parents. Again!"

Uh-oh.

That afternoon when I got home, my mom was frowning. "Your teacher said you were disturbing the class again."

"I didn't mean to," I said. "I just move and talk before my brain can tell me to stop."

Mom kept frowning. "Yesterday you smacked your sister for no reason. Last week you had a huge meltdown at the grocery store and embarrassed me. You run and jump on the couch like it's a trampoline. You never stop moving, and you tire me out. We need to do something. I'm calling the doctor."

I didn't want to go to the doctor. I didn't feel sick, and I was scared I'd have to get a shot.

Dr. Rogers told me I was right – I wasn't sick, and I didn't need a shot. But she gave me some other tests, like standing still on one foot. That was hard for me. She asked if I had trouble sitting in my chair at school.

"I sure do!" I told her. "Sometimes I slide all the way under my desk. You know what, Dr. Rogers? One time I found old gum stuck under there!"

Dr. Rogers smiled, and said I could go play in the waiting room while she and my parents had a little talk.

Later, Mom and Dad explained some things to me.

"Teddy, your doctor says you have an extra-hard time paying attention and controlling your body movements," Mom said. "That's why you have so much trouble sitting still without talking or moving, and why it's tough to focus on your schoolwork."

Dad said, "Dr. Rogers says it's like you have a rocket-powered brain that has bicycle brakes. Your brain is strong, but sometimes it goes so fast that it's difficult for you to focus or to stop before you act. The good news is there are lots of things we can all do to help you."

I decided I like having a rocket-powered brain.

But I wondered if there was something wrong with me. Mom and Dad smiled and hugged me. "No, honey, you're our Terrific Teddy and you're just the way you're supposed to be," Mom said. "The doctor just helped us understand that certain things are harder for you, like thinking before you act and concentrating on things that are boring to you. We just need to start doing a few things differently to help our family."

Well, we started doing a whole lot of things differently. Not just me, but Mom and Dad and my sister, Emily.

We eat a lot less junk food and more protein, whatever that is. Now I even take a vitamin.

I get lots of time after school to run around and ride my bike and climb trees. I still get to play video games, but only a little – and only when my homework is done.

When we go someplace, Mom and Dad remind me and Emily how we're supposed to behave. That helps.

My bedtime is earlier. I didn't like that at all, but I got used to it. Now I feel rested in the morning.

Mom and Dad talked to my teacher, too. She helped me at school, and now I can stand up and work when I feel wiggly. Sometimes I choose to sit at the back table. A lot of things are written down to help me remember.

"With all these changes, school should start getting better for you, and I think we'll be happier as a family, too," Dad told me. "If not, we'll go see Dr. Rogers again, because some kids take medicine to help them. Meanwhile, you'll always be our Terrific Teddy."

I really love my family and my teacher and how much everyone is trying to help me.

I just had one question.

"Do I still have to go to school tomorrow?"

My head knows I do … but the rest of me doesn't always want to!

Optional ending #1:

A lot of famous people have had difficulty controlling their energy, just like Teddy and ... maybe even Albert Einstein, one of the most famous scientists ever!

Optional ending #2:

My parents told me there's a name for the problems I have with self-control and paying attention. It's called Attention Deficit Hyperactivity Disorder. Some people just use the letters ADHD or ADD. Having ADD means you have difficulty concentrating on school or homework, unless it's a topic you're really interested in. Some children with ADD can be extra-forgetful. Other kids with ADHD are hyperactive and impulsive, and they do and say things without thinking ahead. They have difficulty controlling their body and move around a lot. They have problems standing still in line, or they'll shout out in class ... just like I did. The doctor said some kids take medication to help manage their ADHD. Medication can help kids concentrate and think before they act.

People with ADHD may struggle in some areas, but have strengths in other areas that help them excel in life. It's OK to have ADHD, and you can have ADHD and do almost any job. In fact, there are lots of grownups with ADHD who are actors, doctors, lawyers, judges, writers, teachers, mechanics, athletes, and who work for themselves. Some historians think that some super-smart people, like Albert Einstein, may have had ADHD.

About the Author

Jim Forgan, Ph.D., is a licensed school psychologist and professor. In his private practice he evaluates children for dyslexia; reading problems; dyscalculia (math problems); dysgraphia (writing problems); ADHD/ADD; processing problems; learning issues; and social-emotional disorders, such as anxiety, depression, and opposition. Dr. Forgan and his associates also offer services for helping families help children.

Dr. Forgan is married with two children. He understands learning differences not only from a professional perspective, but as the parent of a child with learning differences.

Find additional resources at
www.TerrificTeddy.com

Additional Titles by Jim Forgan, Ph.D.

Raising Boys with ADHD: Secrets for Parenting Healthy, Happy Sons

This book empowers parents to help their sons with ADHD find success in school and beyond. It covers topics not typically found in parenting guides, such as early diagnosis and strategies for teens transitioning to work and college. Written with Mary Anne Richey.

Raising Girls with ADHD: Secrets for Parenting Healthy, Happy Daughters

ADHD in a girl often manifests differently than it does in a boy. This book provides resources to help parents address their daughters' treatment, behavioral strategies, personal/social adjustment and other issues, from preschool through high school. Written with Mary Anne Richey.

The Disorganized, Impulsive Child: Solutions for Parenting Kids with Executive Functioning Difficulties

Children who can't select, plan, initiate, or sustain action toward their goals are children who struggle to succeed in school and other aspects of life. Using the proven advice, interactive surveys and action plans in this book, parents can learn to teach a disorganized, impulsive child to achieve independence, success, and a level of self-support. Written with Mary Anne Richey.

Teaching Problem Solving Through Children's Literature

General and special education teachers will find 40 ready-to-use lesson plans that feature characters from children's literature. Students learn independence in solving problems in their own lives, as well as problem-solving strategies that can be applied to any situation.

Phonics in Lessons, Pictures, and Activities

Help beginning readers sound out words through 48 fully developed lesson plans. Word games, art projects, poems, word scrambles, flashcards, and many more fun activities appear on illustrated, reproducible handouts. The first 30 pages of the book provide teachers (or parents) with a crash course in teaching word sounds and assessing progress. Written with Harry Forgan.

Made in the USA
Middletown, DE
17 June 2016